BOOKS BY ROD McKUEN

POETRY

STANYAN STREET & OTHER SORROWS
LISTEN TO THE WARM
LONESOME CITIES
IN SOMEONE'S SHADOW
CAUGHT IN THE QUIET
FIELDS OF WONDER
MOMENT TO MOMENT
BEYOND THE BOARDWALK
AND TO EACH SEASON . . .
COME TO ME IN SILENCE

PRIVATE EDITIONS

AND AUTUMN CAME
A MAN ALONE

CHRISTMAS POEMS & LYRICS

TWELVE YEARS OF CHRISTMAS
THE CAROLS OF CHRISTMAS

COLLECTED POEMS

WITH LOVE

COLLECTED LYRICS

NEW BALLADS
PASTORALE
THE SONGS OF ROD MCKUEN
GRAND TOUR

COME TO ME IN SILENCE

come to me in silence

ROD McKUEN

CHEVAL BOOKS
—
SIMON AND
SCHUSTER
—
NEW YORK

Published by Simon and Schuster
Rockefeller Center, 630 Fifth Avenue
New York, New York 10020
and Cheval Books
8440 Santa Monica Boulevard
Los Angeles, California 90069

SBN 671-21633-3 Regular edition
SBN 671-21668-6 Deluxe edition
Library of Congress Catalog Card Number: 73-9095
Manufactured in the United States of America
By The Book Press, Brattleboro, Vt.

1 2 3 4 5 6 7 8 9 10

This book is for nobody / everybody

CONTENTS

SEVEN ON A SUMMER BEACH

For Wes Kuney and Newt Eades

1.

Wes the learner made mistakes
but with his youth to cushion him
he always fell to safety.

Murphy's plumber tools were shiny.
Every other week he went,
coming back on even weeks
to tell us how his time was spent.

Bill believed in nothing
except the pots and bowls and busts
that he could conjure out of clay
with his own hands.

2.

Others in our circle.
Newt who tried to be a poet
and with his dying finally was.
Buck with all the morals of a rabbit.
In his head a haunted house
locked with secret secrets to this day.

Lenny lived above the boardwalk
and cooked all day
lending me his room two blocks away,
teaching me while he was there,
leaving me to learn alone when he was gone.

3.

Seven on a summer beach
that stretched the length
                of Santa Monica.
Sunday to Sunday we lived
seventeen summers ago.

Even then my songs were starting
to be only those
of my invention,
made for me
and my small audience
                of friends.

4.

The next song coming
I would always breathe up
from the bottom of my belly
            with all the air I had.

Out of the army, out of work,
I was trained for nothing,
not even the saying of words
or the singing of songs.
But dreams are cheap enough to come by
and I had store fronts full of those.

5.

Dream I did
along that Sunday beach
and then sun saturated
joined the others in the bar.
My unemployment checks now gone
Bill always bought the beer
I nursed the first two hours
till some new friend would buy another.

Ten years later each time we met
he still reminded me that in my early life
he'd been St. Benefactor of The Beer.

6.

Of the seven
Bill was first to marry.
None of us expected it
but all of us were pleased
                        and proud.
By then the two of us
had passed from being friends.
After all, I'd sponged
and in his mind was winning.
What I wondered then.
What I wonder now.

I hope that in Bill's union
there are no guilty parties.

7.

Lenny goes on cooking
                 for all I know.
Probably the chef supreme
with apprentices of every kind.

I hope he's teaching them
all the lessons he taught me,
truths so valuable and ingrained
I'd be hard pressed to call them up
or list them one on one by name.

He called once when I was gone.

There are those who've told
                 and tell me
I've been gone some time.

8.

Murphy went on drinking
till half a glass at evening
became a bottle, finally two.
And evening started on awakening
and ended when he went to sleep.
Not long ago he drifted back,
came into town and stayed a time,
then like his rusty plumber's tools
                       was gone.
I think the only one he saw was Wes.

9.

Even now the horror
of Murphy's gentle giant head
shot through with shot-glass webbing
is hard for me to understand.
I'll never know his like again
      if I even knew it then.

Buck went back to Indiana.
He wrote me once to say
the hunting wasn't great but good
and shouldn't I come there
and shouldn't I give up the city
and be another country Robin Hood?

10.

One year Newt sent out a Christmas card
that showed him taking one long walk
along our old familiar beach.
Printed on it was a paragraph that said
here there is a tree
I want some unborn child to see.

Some years later he was dead,
cut down by person or persons
yet unknown to anyone but him.

11.

I grieve for him
because I always promised
                     him and me
that if I made it
I'd find an audience somewhere
for all the things I knew he'd write.
He left no will and all his poetry
is still locked in the ground
                     inside his head.
Sure wasn't much of a funeral,
even the flowers were dying.
                     He said that too.
And I remember further
that all he asked from any friend
was *a patchwork quilt of hope.*

12.

Wes and I are left.
         Two from seven.
Our lives could not be
more different / more alike.
Passing forty in the same
         two-month span,
we've both grown beards.
We both have semisteady hands.
Each of us is bored with beaching
and the wasted time it takes
         to cultivate a tan.
I like him better now
we have a kinship, having both survived

13.

Married life
wears well on him,
he's fatter and he laughs
and finally he's that little boy
he used to such perfection
back when he was just another one of us
shaking sand from out his socks
and following friendly enemies
everywhere and home.

If I smile too much
my friend corrects my grin
but I love Wes enough now
to find no single thing in him
                    to censure.

14.

That leaves *me*.

I am where I left off
a month, an hour ago.
My lament is yet unwritten
                    therefore still not sung.
It does not come up from my stomach
                              easily.
Could I put it into one long line
I'd have to say that what I longed for
                    knowing it or not
is out there somewhere out of reach
and day by day, week by week,
I lose the Jason urge to start the chase.

15.

It may be
the one I have imagined
            or imagine not
will, on some quiet afternoon
                  or silent night
when this old house resounds
or fails to echo with the small noise
            I make on my own,
finding this place, know enough
to come in slowly, unafraid
and share with me a certain kind
                        of silence.

COME TO ME IN SILENCE

Entry I: SILENCE

Ivy geranium has sped across the front end of the yard, strangling the dandelion and the rose alike. Flowering now in pink and white and almost red, it hides its tentacles. Still, you know that inch by inch underground and just above, it slowly moves to capture this whole block. I doubt the hedge will offer much resistance. The ivy is an idea that has found its time April into June. Three months should be enough to see it do its final battle. One last all-out offensive and every foot of ground will be geranium, made so in silence—no evidence of proper plan.

So much is done in silence. So much accomplished without word. I read silence like a Bible, attend it like a reference work. Having tasted it with the well-loved, making love, and the would-be lover after loving didn't work.

Silence is the science of the times that stay. And yet we use whole paragraphs to say what saying nothing could have spoken better.

INVOCATION

I do not doubt
that in some hidden
            middle night
you'll rise up
and come to me
in solitude or silence.

We will meet
as we have met
on a train or at the end
of some new train of thought.

COME TO ME IN SILENCE

Come to me in silence
out of the noise of noon.
Be the eye inside of me.
Help me drink the river up
          and swallow it,
or let me take great mouthfuls
             out of you,
stampeding you to bed
and then beyond,
             beyond.

I do not expect
that we will meet again
in the same way as before,
you freckled by the summer morning
            smiling like a china cup over blue-white
            gingham.
Me blue-jeaned and apple-cheeked
a frown away from being glad.
Accept the fact that we will grow
perhaps in different ways.

Come to me in solitude
pushing through the crowd
there are no others here
to pry or make demands.
If no one waits for you
                    but me,
I wait in that same solitude
that brings you here.

Come to me in silence
like the land-bound stone
pushed and shoved
    and finally sailed
against the gray indifferent shore.

Prophecies I have
and I am not indifferent
only gray,
full of dark midwinter questions
some that none could know or guess.

WIND SONG

Moths
fill up the morning
and spiders slide down
shafts of sunlight.

The wind now makes
a long, slow moan
tired of all the old Octobers,
weary of the ones ahead,
the moan is more a sigh.

Resigned
like those of us
who face the wind
the wind itself looks up,
and seeing autumn,
runs to hide.

NEW DIRECTIONS

If I hold my hand
in front of me
            just so
it covers up the moon.

I can move
from block to block
clearheaded, unafraid.
If I haven't charted out
the action in advance.

Premeditation
is the surest enemy
                I know.

Slow
I move my hand away
uncovering the moon.
          Slower still
Small thoughts widen
and stretch out in my head.

The moon draws nearer.

Frightened now
        and running,
chased block to block
by that white moon
I strike out for yesterday
sure that if my feet
run far and fast enough
I'll never reach tomorrow.

MINUS ONE

I would travel
out of love
if that way
was any way but long.

Tired
of endless journeys
it seems
more simple
   and more sure
not to move at all.

Whatever the arithmetic
the end of love is slow
and which of us
is bright enough
to not begin
that longest of all journeys
                    that starts
with every new encounter
and seldom ends
with every new beginning?

BY THE NUMBERS

You went away
in such great numbers.

A covey of you
at the corner.
A band of you
beyond the block.
A herd of you
unhearing as I cried aloud,
come back, come back.

You went away so often
and in such great numbers
that I'd not be surprised
to meet a regiment of you
clicking down the sidewalk
clacking up the street
returning, coming back.

TURNING POINT

The road turns here,
up ahead you see it
dissolving in the dust.

I would have you now
dissolving into me
suspended,
        held aloft
by my arms only.
Hanging on but letting go.

The sky is cloudless here
look above and you can see it
blue on blue, bareheaded
          and not breathing.
I would wish from you
          the same clear
               cloudless eye
seeking mine straightforwardly
                    and true
not breathing and bareheaded
as I breathe my way through you.

The sun is friendly here
look just left and you can see it
warm but kindly so and clearly caring.
I would ask of you
        that you be ever warm
willing to be kind
not letting me forget that kindness
is the passport and the proven way
for two to journey through a lifetime,
each other, or a single summer day.

THEY

They are meeting in rooms
or turning in hallways.
They make covenants
in countries not known to me.
They poison the air
with their pride in each other.
They foul the night
with their gratified desires.

They muddle me
by passing past me
not noticing my need
pretending not to recognize
the hope that happens
              on my face
when one of them goes by.
They insult me
by insisting on each other.
They kill me with the care
they show their own.

They devour me by degrees
and I let them.

COLORADO SUNDAYS

For Pat Hanna

Entry II: COLORADO

Rain in Denver is dependable. Summer month or Spring. Every day at five o'clock you can set your watch by when it starts to rain. At three the sky burns brown. By four it deepens into umber. Finally at five, prearranged, predictable, a small rain, never out of reason, starts. You would think monsoons had come the way the Colorado heaven carries on. So much drumming up of thunder, so much flashing hill to hill. In the end the rain is always small. Not hard enough to twist umbrellas, but wet enough to wash the sidewalk down and rivulet in every gutter.

Sometimes on Sundays there's a special rain. More a mist. One Sunday out of twelve, the rain sleeps late. If it hasn't come by five, it doesn't come at all.

SUNDAY ONE

I have no doubt
that Indian paintbrush
flower on the Colorado hills
all spring and summer long.
And these same aspen
lifeless now and leafless
in the cool pre-winter
could not I know
have been as beautiful
rouged and rainbowed
as they were
in last week's autumn.

Knowing this October day
will not repeat itself
we roll a while longer
on the cold damp earth
a mile above Georgetown.
Reckless in an open field
seen by anyone
savoring this same Sunday
in this same Sunday place.
Innocent we are
but not to any eyes
            but ours.

Good Sam
goes plodding through
the brush ahead
not noticing
     but taking notice
only just enough
to give us the horizon's edge
as he moves down into a gully,
not looking back
but pretending to be
plotting out or plodding down
        a new path.

Now eye to eye
and heavy lidded,
till you force a smile from me
that crumples up the silence.

One more breath from you
            against my own
might have brought
a loss of innocence
giving us a gain of greatness.

I hope I never smile again
for after coming up
through almost forty years
I was but a breath away
from new breath
and new life.
But innocent I am
and will remain
of your body melting
                    into mine.

Why you stopped the lightning
              I can't say,
but Sam as he returned
careful to make noise
amid the underbrush,
and thus be heard,
looked as though
he'd tasted thunder.

SUNDAY TWO

I wish for you
Sweet Sunday psalms
and carols of an evening,
sung out clear and strong,
coming up from chests
you haven't lain against just yet—
but will.

I wish you free,
face down in every lap that walked away
without your head pressed hard
against its Venus mound or crotch.

Surprising you midsentence
                              unsuspectingly
caring and carrying you carefully
to his own—your own Eden.

I wish you vintage wine
in every Coca-Cola glass

an end to wishing
signaling you've found forever
at the end of now.

Could I command your mouth
to talk at my ear only
and climb on my mouth every time
you know I would and more.

I'd wish beyond all reason.
Because I want
              beyond all want
                         for you.

I would wish for you the world
if it were good enough for you,
each morning sky
                    hanging
                    out
                        there
                    clear as crystal.
I'd reel in for you
and doing so, make real.

SUNDAY THREE

We cannot go both ways
though I know you'll try.
I could take you up one road
            and down another,
but one Sunday middle-month
is not enough to start a trip,
let alone do a journey justice.

So we meet and part
and maybe meet again,
lonesome travelers hiking
up some hill of hope
then down a Denver Sunday
at the summer's start.
I don't know where I am.
            Do you?

SOUTHERN CALIFORNIA SUNDAYS

Entry III: CALIFORNIA

What death cannot dictate and life cannot insure, a single California Sunday works out easily, the winding down of weekday will.

Convertibles fornicate on freeways, play chicken at the off-ramps, or late at night, engage big-wheelers in the light game—trying, I suppose, to milk the last few weekend hours. Beaches are not beaches anymore, they are Times Square crowds on New Year's Eve, spectators at a stadium or huddled masses yearning to breathe free on one large blanket stretching all the way from Malibu to Zuma.

On Olivera Street, the women left to dress the saints congregate to gossip and to giggle. Some I know still make the "milk run" from L.A. to points south—Long Beach, El Toro, San Diego, then back again, though passing San Clemente is a problem—or it could be.

My own Sundays are a new joy now. A friend comes visiting and we do nothing, except perhaps to swim and polaroid the sunshine and battle in the bedroom all the weekend. How long this time will last is something neither of us care to think about. But for the moment I'm relaxed, amazing all my friends with my magician-like sereneness.

God grant me absolution for the time I waste, but let me waste some several dozen Sundays more.

SUNDAY ONE

How can I sleep
with owls about
calling
    and recalling?

Bluejay jabberwocky
goes on endlessly.
The low growl
of the dog
comes up rumbling
through the room.
Cats mate and howl
and maybe mate again.

Crickets
if they are about
are smothered
by this orchestration
and behind it all
owls calling and recalling
play their slow and steady bass.

This band now tuning up
impatient for the sunrise
will be too tired to play
          come morning.

SUNDAY TWO

Come now the bright red galleons
chopping through the seas
                    of sensibility.

passing by and passing by

oarsmen at their oars
chained into believing
every voyage has its end,
every chain its weakest link.

That is not so.
The sea's as endless
                        as the end
and galleons
            have been known
to meet themselves
coming round again.

SUNDAY THREE

Dreams run to reality
and once or twice
the marriage works,
though in the end
reality dissolves
completely into dream.

For Jim Teague

SUNDAY FOUR

Twenty minutes
till the clock's
    first shriek.

Alarm uncoiled
coffee boiling
we begin one more
            eventful,
uneventful day.

CHILDREN OF THE SUN

For Skeeter Davis

Entry IV: THEN

Across the street from where we lived in Alamo, a poplar tree was split straight down the middle by a single bolt of lightning. I saw it. I did. A summer evening, thirty years or more ago, an ageless poplar pierced and sliced in half while I sat rocking in the porch swing, wet down by rain. Ever after that, or so it seemed, Grandpa would threaten us with lightning. If we didn't eat our creamed asparagus or boiled codfish, if we set out late for school, chased the chickens or stole tomatoes from the backyard garden, some blue-white flash would sneak up on us and cut us down.

Lightning didn't, doesn't frighten me. Thunder did, does.

Best of all I like the rain their union makes. This summer I hope to build a porch and later on a hammock or a swing.

WINNEMUCCA, NEVADA

The first desk that I had
was big enough to sink down into
and not be observed by teacher
or by pupils in the rows ahead.
My first disguise,
a desk that I could crawl behind
                or under
and become the Scarlet Pimpernel
or Errol Flynn or Walter Mitty
or whatever I became—
someone wonderful
when I felt that I was nothing.

See Dick
see Dick run
and ever after
I'd chase Dicks
                and Daveys
down alleyways
and anywhere,
settling in the end for Spot
or Kelly as I call him,
watching Jane run by.

Jane runs the hardest.
      I've seen her
           leap
              tall
                  buildings
with a single bound,
get tangled in the rigging
as she spied on ships
and come untangled
when she found a friendly one.

Ah, to come upon her
        in the darkness
and find her out an angel
not an angry Amazon
capable of skipping stones
as well as skipping rope.

Oh, to see her
        all together, all together
resting after running,
rolling in toward me
        like a new blue fog.

Run, Jane, run
toward me not away.
Drop your banner
just this once.
I don't insist,
but I suggest
that two can hopscotch
        side by side
if the squares are two feet bigger
and the block one more foot wide.

VACANT LOT

Coming through
the twice-cracked concrete
in the vacant lot next door,
a sprig, not quite a tree
but strong and growing stronger
surviving where a house
                could not survive.
The house was trucked away
                    last summer
board by board and brick by brick.

I never knew the family living there
as I've not had communion
with most communes
                congregated on this street.
Anyway, a sprig—
                not quite a tree
is more sociable than any family
save a family of grass.
Not as friendly
as a well-loved animal,
but equal to the task
of being loved
      and loving.

CHILDREN OF THE SUN

Come home you children of the sun
enter doorways laughing, lingering,
staying for the space of this one
                    afternoon.
Going only when you're summoned
to supper and to sleep.
Coming yet another day
to climb my trees
        and trample down my roses.

Stretch out upon my grass
exercising your young limbs
in the sandlot game.
Come you children of the sun
save all your unsung songs for me.
Take liberties with my front yard.
Laugh at and with me.
Trust me as you trust each other.

That great ball of fire
stumbles now
is sinking fast.
Expecting it to roll
                or stretch
through yet another day
is much too much to ask.
Now come you children
of the yellow sun,
begin your games
within the daylight left.

For Andy Anderson

FLYING IN THE FACE OF GOD

In a biplane once
while flying higher
than I thought I could
I half expected to meet God
behind each cloud
       I passed.
God with the face
of Father Christmas
would be smiling
or frowning with a frown
      I bet I knew.

We didn't meet
but that is not to say
we didn't touch
or that we didn't
        pass by close.

I have the courage now
to one day fly
through air so thin
only God could live there
                with any certainty.

If I fall back down again
a hand of sure direction
will have pushed me.

TOO LATE TO MATTER

Entry V: TOO LATE

Some words come too late to matter. A phone call never made. A letter put away lost, unanswered. A meeting and a dialogue not done. Recriminations go on ringing through our heads when we've missed an only chance and words come out of us like bullets when the time is gone.

We lose a chapter and a chance because of hesitation or made-up appointment.

Even when I know the promises I'm making won't be kept I tell one more tomorrow I'll be there. Later, late for the appointment, the words flow easily.

UNANSWERED

I put off writing
then to find
you'd put off living
in the interval.

I have no excuse.
My arm well oiled
and still working
could have written
half a page or more.

While we were living
face to face,
I was willing once
to use you
as a sounding board.
You were my acoustic then.
You shame me now.

That I would let your letter
                    go unanswered
is a loss to me
and not a lesson.

For Meade Parks

SANDBURG FIELD / FLAT ROCK

The goats come running
down the hill and to the gate
the kids on wobbly legs behind.
I stand still a minute
and look out across
the spring-green Sandburg field,
Lincolnlike and lonely.

The house behind me
　　　　where he lived
is quiet now and empty
but for books and books
　　　　　　　and books,
　　　　　　magazines and books.
Lap shawl on the wall
hanging limp
not altogether lifeless,
and in another room some books.

Here he walked
        or didn't walk.
Here he came and stood,
looking out across
as if his eyes would take him
                        out beyond
this same green field
interrupted as I am just now
by goats that nibble at my knuckles
and kids that stand in line behind.

EASTER WEEK REMEMBERED

Two years less a week
that you've been gone.
How have I come this far
and how do I go on
             without you?

The night continues
birds bark outside
instead of dogs
and I have not been
             sleeping.

Is it fair
that you sleep
through eternity
                untroubled
while I am left
alive, awake
to trouble over
why you sleep?

April
and I leave again
already looking up ahead
to the June return.

Though I come back
to this place alone
            to nothing,
least of all
the certainty of sleep,
I count cadence
till the June return.

I box my papers
lock the cupboards
that have locks
 (though they contain
no tricks or treasures,
no secrets secret any more).
I fold and hide away
those things that need to be
folded up and hidden.

Sure
that what life
I am leaving here
will not be molested
sorted out or shuffled through.
I snap my suitcase shut
and travel down
the April morning
            to start
the new spring tour.

PICASSO

You drew a woman's hills
and openings so well
the blueprint
must have come
from God himself.

THE COWARD AS HERO

Some heroes
leave behind
a line to live by.

This one said
if love were all

SEVERAL KINDS OF SNOW

Entry VI: SNOW

I've tried to make an "entry" out of snow. It melts as quickly as it's put to paper. Why I wonder? Denver winters are a fact of life. Amsterdam has turned my ear a dozen kinds of red in as many years. Just how the snow came down in Washington and Edmonton and Portland, long ago, is easily remembered.

London: when the first flake falls half the city's given to pretending it's the first time ever. Therein lies the clue. Like a half-forgotten joke, surprises lose their awe, relived, retold.

If I could talk with truth about Detroit, or all those years in Elko, I'd have fantasies and truths to fill a volume, but snow melts in the telling.

For Hans Kellerman

THE SNOWS OF AMSTERDAM

You can almost hear
the snow fall down
      in Amsterdam.
It comes with such a force
that people in the streets
bend forward weighted down
          like trees.
They shield themselves
like frightened deer
ducking doorway to doorway
till they're safely home.

Diligent and evenly
the snow now covers
every street and sidewalk.
Nothing's left to chance
                    as slowly
through the near-deserted town
the clouds unlock their fists
and let the snow fall down.

The ground is now
all winter white
not Pendleton
but sheet white
    like a made-up bed.
The clouds have done their job.
But who's to say where God's cloud ends
and the snows of Amsterdam begin.

WINTER ALTERNATIVE

Without the sun's sure passion
or rain in friendly autumn
fashioning a need for us,
and no red bedrooms
double-decked with flowers
we'll stay alone in winter.

Our skins white
as any snowflake
and whiter still than any
overhanging bower
weighted down with snow.

Because we need to fill
this time now empty
and as endless
as the worn-out winter
we'll use a cold lock
in the same way
we might have been dependent on
embraces in another season.

Here in this snowy stillness
where there has so long been
an absence of reality
you must make some sense for me,
forcing fact into my life
more true than trumped-up fiction
but every bit as full and free.

I charge you
with invention for me
I trust you to make over
what needs making over.

A FIST FULL OF SNOW

I need from you
suspension,
absolution of a kind.
A now that turns
       into an always,
but first some rethink time.

We must know each other
       free and freely
the way we both pretend we do.

Your bowels and brains
must be as sure for me
as both my eyes.
Your neck
as near remembered
as a home-town atlas.

Because I need familiars
I need you as a fact,
An absolute and not an act.

Passing through the sheets
and climbing down inside of you
even though you give back
one for one and more
some questions linger *still*
                    as questions.
Have I traversed
or gone climbing
down a shaft so new
that none, not even I
have charted it before.

Have we been apart so long
that there's no getting back?
Was there a curve
we didn't go around together,
one embankment one of us
            did not foresee?
Worse—has someone else
been hiking down your highway?

Change is change
unaccountable
but nonetheless surprising.
I had hoped
all our surprises
would be planned
            together.

There is
some silence here
like dead wood
        in the wood.
Moving only
        when it's prodded.
Silence made of snow.
The way the early summer
is constructed out of rain.

This quiet is not of easy making,
but necessary all the same.

You move off
and I'm stopped still
arms akimbo, open wide
one tight fist remains,
contracting and expanding,
expanding and contracting
full of snow
full of water/full of snow.

ROD McKUEN was born in Oakland, California, and has traveled extensively throughout the world both as a concert artist and a writer. In less than five years six of his books of poetry have sold nearly eight million copies in hard cover, making him the best-selling and most widely read poet of all times. In addition he is the best-selling living author writing in any hard-cover medium today. His poetry is taught and studied in schools, colleges, universities and seminaries throughout the world, and the author spends a good deal of his time visiting and lecturing on campus.

Mr. McKuen is also the composer of more than 1,000 songs that have been translated into Spanish, French, Dutch, German, Russian, Czechoslovakian, Japanese, Chinese, Norwegian and Italian, among other languages. They account for the sale of more than one hundred million records. His film music has twice been nominated for Motion Picture Academy Awards.

Rod McKuen's classical music, including symphonies, concertos, piano sonatas and his very popular Adagio for Harp & Strings, is performed by leading orchestras in the United States and

throughout Europe. In May of 1972, the Royal Philharmonic Orchestra in London premiered his Concerto #3 for Piano & Orchestra, and an orchestral suite, The Plains of My Country.

Before becoming a best-selling author and composer, Mr. McKuen worked as a laborer, radio disc jockey and newspaper columnist. Of his military service during and after the Korean War, the author says, "I was a private in the army who rose from that rank once only to descend rather swiftly."

The author makes his home in California in a rambling Spanish house which he shares with a menagerie of Old English sheep dogs and eight cats. He likes outdoor sports and driving. He has just completed an extensive book about the sea and is currently editing and assembling the first definitive collection of the words and music to more than fifty of his most popular songs. Both books will be published by Simon and Schuster.

"The Snows of Amsterdam" first appeared in the Stanyan album, "Amsterdam Concert," in slightly different form.